Mental Health Ministry for Churches

Mental Health Ministry for Churches

A Handbook for Getting Started or to Supplement Current Programs

Marcia A. Murphy

RESOURCE *Publications* • Eugene, Oregon

MENTAL HEALTH MINISTRY FOR CHURCHES
A Handbook for Getting Started or to Supplement Current Programs

Resource Publications
An Imprint of Wipf and Stock Publishers
199 W. 8th Ave., Suite 3
Eugene, OR 97401

www.wipfandstock.com

PAPERBACK ISBN: 979-8-3852-7649-3
HARDCOVER ISBN: 979-8-3852-7650-9
EBOOK ISBN: 979-8-3852-7651-6

VERSION NUMBER 04/02/26

Contents

Introduction

You are the salt of the earth...

You are the light of the world. A city set on a hill cannot be hid. Nor do men light a lamp and put it under a bushel, but on a stand, and it gives light to all in the house. Let your light so shine before men, that they may see your good works and give glory to your Father who is in heaven.

—Matthew 5:13a,14–16 RSV

Religious communities are called to be salt and light to the surrounding civic communities which, in themselves, contribute talents and gifts accordingly. When we have both segments working together in tandem, this is a winning proposition. And when the subject matter is mental health churches have a vital role in coordinating new and improved ways to serve the ill, their families, and places of work.

As humans are body, mind, and spirit, to leave out one aspect of health is crippling. As a way to increase awareness of the ways to improve mental and emotional health, Saint Andrew Presbyterian church (USA) of Iowa City, Iowa, established programs to serve the purpose of improving the lives of those with mental afflictions and to assist their families. This handbook has been based on the successful work of team leaders for mental health ministries at St. Andrew. This book will describe the events and activities that will strengthen the mental health of not only the individual lives of congregants in a church setting, but also the surrounding community, as well as region, states, nation, and world.

Written by a person who is, herself, in recovery from mental illness, the author provides insights and ideas that come from someone who has experienced the devastation of psychiatric affliction and who can thereby identify what is most helpful.

This handbook is a valuable tool and resource to implement changes in spiritual and mental health that will affect hundreds, if not, thousands of lives, for the better. This resource can be used to start new programs, or it can be a guide to supplement what already exists as an organization's current mental health ministry.

There are two valuable branches that work alongside of each other for St. Andrew's mental health ministries each led by different people who have different gifts and talents.

I

Minds Matter

Team leaders: Amy Schmidt-Rundell, Nichole Hoffman
St. Andrew Presbyterian Church, Iowa City, Iowa US

An Interview with Amy Schmidt-Rundell and Nichole Hoffman

AMY SCHMIDT-RUNDELL IS A wife and mother of seven, along with her position as staff at St. Andrew Presbyterian Church as Mission and Outreach Coordinator, and Building Use Coordinator. Though a hearing person, herself, Amy is also profluent in American Sign Language (ASL).

Nichole Hoffman, wife, and mother of two, is a part of a team of directors for St. Andrew Presbyterian Church Children's and Family Ministries. Previously trained as a social worker, she filled various positions in the healthcare field, along with working as a paraprofessional with children in schools.

How did Minds Matter get started?:

A church committee was questioning what would the next new program be for St. Andrew. We started with just getting together and conversing about it and making a plan. We like to have the mental health event in the fall and since we live in a college town, we had to make sure our event wasn't scheduled on the same day as a football game because of the large number of people who follow football. We really like having our event in November. That seems to be a good time, shortly after kids come back to school here in Iowa City and also just before all the holidays hit really hard.

How did you form your Minds Matter team?

We have a small committee of about ten people. Currently they're all from our church but we are looking at expanding that because our goal is to have people from our community and experiences beyond our own to help us to keep improving our event. There is another church that I'll be reaching out to as they also have a mental health focus. We'd like to collaborate with them some more and between the two, hopefully can reach more people in church communities. Our focus is not the church, itself, our focus is for mental health and the importance of making sure people can learn about opportunities in our community and corridor area.

So how did you choose speakers for your Mind Matter events and what kind of topics do you look for?

The first year we had it we invited someone who uses humor when talking about mental health. She does it in a way that is not so scary because a lot of people just don't even know what to think, there's such stigma with mental health so we wanted to have somebody that could kind of break the ice.

And then we also had someone who does a lot of advocacy at the state level trying to pass bills so she came and spoke to us also as well as having personal experience with her own family And then we've also had a professor that has come and spoken to us.

We don't really have a specific type of person we're looking for. We're looking for people who are passionate about the topic, and who have a willingness to share. People who are advocates for mental health.

We had a speaker who focused on youth and generations and another who spoke about all the opportunities in our area and she was full of information.

We don't necessarily have specific people to find. What we do is look for people who have a passion either from personal experience or if it's from a professional side of things.

We put a notice out in our church newsletter announcing that we were going to be having a team for mental health and asked who would like to join?

Then as we've had events more people have joined if they've just helped for the day and have enjoyed being a part of that. The volunteers that helped us with the events are the same committee members that the team has. Sometimes we have some people outside of our team that help doing the prep with food or things like that or help with the logistics of those things and we're very appreciative of them. But the majority of it is on the day of the event we all take a role and go to work. Often, Nichole is a greeter; I (Amy) usually help set things up and do the logistics of everything and then we have other people from our team that are the ones that help oversee the kitchen or things like that.

ADDITIONAL INFORMATION

The tables in the large atrium of the church is where numerous organizations that support or advocate for mental health are set up. In the large room next to it, there is the craft fair. At the craft fair people pay a fee to have their own table and this money goes into paying the fee for the speakers at Minds Matter. Not all speakers request compensation, but for those that do, the income from the craft fair supports this. Craft makers are allowed to keep the profits from their own sales of their crafts.

Sometimes people have asked why the Minds Matter event isn't held downtown. The answer is that when held downtown, there are large fees to use facilities.

As far as marketing for Minds Matter, at times, the leaders are asked to participate in radio and TV shows. Producers will attend outdoor city pedestrian mall events where organizations are set up and extend invitations to be on their shows. Also flyers are put up all over town and ads are placed in newspaper-type papers. The church will put ads in their newsletters, as well as at the Presbytery level.

The feedback forms received give tips for how to arrange things for the following year's events. For example, the hours for the event and time of year and what speakers were helpful and most interesting. Amy and Nichole contact potential speakers by email or phone. In addition to speakers, they have a panel of authors who've written about their experience with mental health and related issues. The authors discuss their books and accept questions from the audience.

Amy and Nichole have been exemplary church workers in their examples of organizing the Minds Matter church events along with their core volunteers. The integrity of character within their personalities along with their kind-hearted and genuine warmth, is like a magnet drawing in individuals to participate who come from every walk of life. People come from different faiths or from no faith background, and they are welcomed with open arms. Minds Matter is a cultural event that is inclusive and brings together resources in the forms of people and organizations who truly care about each other. When you have people who care about each other, this is a winning proposition. Healing happens. Amy and Nichole, the leaders of Minds Matter, have tirelessly driven forward the message that help is out there and when you come to a Minds Matter event you can be introduced to it, supported, and guided. Hundreds of individuals are involved in the presenting and receiving end. This social interaction is possibly live-saving for those who previously felt there was no hope. Connections are made and information is shared. "A new commandment I give to you, that you love one another; even as I have loved you, that you also love one another. By this all men will know that you are my disciples, if you have love for one another." (John 13: 34–35 RSV)

II

Mental Health Initiatives (MHI)

Founder and team leader: Marcia A. Murphy
St. Andrew Presbyterian Church, Iowa City, Iowa, US

Mental Health Initiatives (MHI) was founded in 1997 by Marcia A. Murphy. Its mission is to promote the dignity, value, and inherent worth of people who live with mental illness. To advocate through educational means, as well as provide practical, psychological, and social support for the mentally ill, the most neglected and marginalized members of society. MHI is a strong advocate for people either abled or disabled. It works at identifying and promoting the role of hope and health in improving relationships in family, in society, in self-care, and in wellness. There are numerous initiatives created by MHI which focus on this mission.

MHI is in many ways a boots on the ground inner-city outreach: to show compassion to those afflicted with mental illness and by providing practical resources to the mentally ill homeless through hands on, one-on-one encounters, and creating drop-in centers. Provides support for homeless individuals by providing food to individuals on the streets, along with emotional support, advocacy, friendship, clothing, and money. MHI partners with homeless shelters. "When the Son of man comes in his glory, and all the angels with him, then he will sit on his glorious throne. Before him will be gathered all the nations, and he will separate them one from another as a shepherd separates the sheep from the goats, and he will place the sheep at his right hand, but the goats at the left. Then the King will say to those at his right hand, 'Come, O blessed of my Father, inherit the kingdom prepared for you from the foundation of the world; for I was hungry and you gave me food, I was thirsty and you gave me drink, I was a stranger and you welcomed me, I was naked and you clothed me, I was sick and you visited me, I was in prison and you came to me.' Then the righteous will answer him, 'Lord, when did we see thee hungry and feed thee, or thirsty and give thee drink? And when did we see thee a stranger and welcome thee, or naked and clothe thee? And when did we see thee sick or in prison and visit thee?' And the King will answer them, 'Truly, I say to you, as you did it to one of the least of these my brethren, you did it to me. (Matt 25: 31–40 RSV)

MHI team members assist the homeless by providing shelter and food. Some homeless persons are taken care of by church members within the members' homes. If they need clothes and shoes the church provides these necessities. The church has also purchased jackets and warm winter coats. The homeless are invited to attend worship services in the church, itself. Some homeless individuals find much comfort and solace there. Being around kind people is helpful for the homeless to regain some mental health. The music during worship services is soothing and brings healing. Because not only do the mentally ill sometimes become homeless, but the experience of homelessness, itself, makes a person mentally ill. Having no safe place to sleep, being out in the cold or summer's stifling heat, can destroy one's mental health. Not having enough food to eat, daily, the extreme hunger, causes mental illness. And the rejection from business leaders when kicked out of coffee shops or stores, and society in general, causes mental illness. The extreme temperatures of sub-zero F degree weather will kill some of the homeless and the extreme heat in the summer, can also kill. The mentally ill are desperate people. MHI team members recognize this and go into the city with money, and sandwiches, bottles of water and juice and give freely to those in need.

The homeless, many of them, enjoy a conversation, to share how their day is going and where they slept the night before. One homeless man has an injured foot and he is able to access medical care at a nearby hospital. There they do wound care and apply a boot on his foot. Thie medical care is life-saving because of possible infections. Marcia became interested in helping the poor partially due to her own lifetime circumstances. Being estranged from a difficult biological family and then physically, separated from the home, she at many points in her life, was without security of a place to live and often was without adequate food supplies. Many times, she relied on a friend or abusive boyfriend to provide a roof over her head. Once she had an apartment but the heating system broke down in the dead of winter and she would have died from cold exposure and so a man she was dating allowed her to live temporarily with him until the heating system was repaired. But he physically and emotionally abused her. Marcia cried out, "There is no place on earth for me!" Justice, and only justice, you shall follow, that you may live and inherit the land which the Lord your God gives you. (Deut 16:20 RSV)

So this personal experience of homelessness and deprivation gave Marcia insight and compassion for others who suffer in a similar way. People often criticize the homeless and accuse them of laziness: "Just get a job!" However, finding work isn't the problem. It's other things causing issues: Where to keep ones extra clothes and belongings when employed. If you leave your things out on the street when you go to your job, it will be stolen while you are away. And how can you find a shower and change of clothes so you can look decent? If you are starving, it is almost impossible to do a hard day's work. People need food in their stomachs to be productive, to have the energy to work. So, feed the poor, so they will have strength to work. Give them places to shower and a place to store their belongings safely. The Housing First movement has the right idea, that a roof over one's head is basic to stability. Many homeless who have substance abuse problems are eager to reform. Give them a chance. Too often the judgment from outsiders is coming from individuals who have no insight into what causes the psychological disfunction among the homeless. People are too busy with sports, or pleasures, or their own issues to reach out and hear the stories from the homeless. If nobody wants to take the time to assist, then the homeless situation in their city will get worse. Once you bring a homeless person inside your own house it soon becomes evident that these people do enjoy working and take part in the household chores. They will sweep and mop the floors, often without being asked to do so. They will wash and dry and put away the dishes. They will scrub everything in the bathroom to make it shiny clean. They will organize the closets. They will take out the trash. They will make the surroundings neat and tidy. They love to work and just need the opportunity to do so. If asked, they will do the grocery shopping getting everything you need listed on a sheet of paper for them. At rest in the home, they enjoy simple things like listening to the radio along with eating some Ramen soup with a glass of milk. Some homeless are eager to read anything they can get their hands on, such as Bibles, nonfiction, and stories. Religion is a big part of some homeless people's lives. If not able to attend worship services, they will often sit outside the church building holding their, "Homeless" cardboard signs. The barriers seem unsurmountable. People forget to be kind to the poor or they are too busy.

MHI was invited to partner with the city's homeless shelter. One day, Marcia was downtown at a restaurant. Looking out the window, she saw an old, rundown building with windows boarded up and spray painted with graffiti. She thought, this building is not in use, it is in the heart of downtown, so why not turn it into a clubhouse drop-in model for the homeless. There they could come in from the cold, or summer's heat. They would find a bathroom, some bottled water, snacks, and place to rest. However, after checking with a county official, Marcia found the city was not interested in using this old building to help the poor, let alone, homeless. Marcia then walked around the city blocks and saw *For Rent* signs in empty store front windows. She wrote down the real estate agents' names and contact information, and later talked to them. What became readily apparent was the high cost of renting a facility in the downtown area. And getting the expenses covered would have taken a miracle. Another roadblock was getting the landlord's permission to rent a space. Landlords didn't want anything to do with the homeless, the poor. They said, *No way!* The agents provided the information regarding the terms of the lease, the requirements for insurance, the down payments, the utility costs, all in addition to the rent fee, and their rules for occupancy. It seemed unsurmountable. Marcia met with some members of the city's homeless shelter and discussed the proposal and subsequent problems associated with it. After a lively discussion, it was concluded that the priority for available funds would be to get the homeless into their own individual homes, first. We wouldn't focus on drop-in centers downtown. Thankfully, a center for seniors was generously allowing many homeless to drop in there, along with a city recreation center opened its doors and shower facilities for the homeless. The public library graciously allowed the poor and homeless to come in on hot summer days and frigid winter days, to rest on its chairs and read books, magazines, and newspapers. The library allows public computer use as well, and it has public restrooms.

BOOKS AND ARTICLES

Marcia writes and publishes books to educate the academic, general public, and care providers on ways to promote healing and recovery for those with mental illness, as well as providing insight into the roadblocks and challenges facing the mentally ill many of whom live in severe poverty. During her early teen years Marcia developed a mental illness. Since then her life has taken many turns, some towards recovery. Marcia has written about her experiences so that the lives of others who have a mental illness might be improved. She hopes that her insights will stimulate new thought concerning the meaning in psychoses, the forces of stigmatization, and the search for survival. Her experiences and perspectives have implications not only for the psychiatrically disabled, but also for those who support the ill: their families, therapists, and physicians. The books and articles Marcia has written are evidence and support for an integrated approach to psychiatric care in treating the body, mind, and spirit. Through her writing she explains how spirituality, alongside of biology and other factors, is an integral part of recovery and is essential for healing the emotional, psychological, and physical suffering inherent in illness. Research has shown that spirituality in particular or, religious faith, play an important role in the recovery process. Marcia intends with her writing to educate, spread awareness, and inform. Marcia's writing ministry began when she received encouragement from her psychiatrist to do the writing many years ago. She had suffered a mental breakdown in her late 30s and nearly succeeded in ending her own life and recovery began when sitting at an old fashioned electric typewriter she typed out the Lord's Prayer. Her faith, it became evident, was the key to stability and the resurrection of her personal life. Often, Marcia felt that without God, she'd be dead. So, she wanted to write about it. Marcia's psychiatrist was a Christian. He also felt that faith in God mattered. As a professor, her psychiatrist had the editorial skills to guide Marcia as she worked. This writing work gave Marcia a sense of purpose, meaning, and psychological healing. It gave her strength. As Marcia's writing became published in professional journals, and later on, full-length books, her audience grew so that socially, Marcia now had more people in her life. You see, stigma can crush a human being to the point of suicide. Someone hears the name of schizophrenic, and all kinds of bad, ugly images come to mind. However, this isn't a multiple personality, it can have to do with a psychotic break or psychosis. Hearing voices most other people do not hear is an isolating experience. So, Marcia wrote about her psychosis, her life of poverty, her search for love in caring relationships, and a decent home.

Churches have a vital role to support the social integration of those afflicted with mental illness. Marcia has written about the struggles of finding a church home. Some people are afraid to get involved. Others show kindness. Marcia's writing stresses the importance of giving the mentally ill a chance. The prayer ministry group of a church plays a big role. And the Deacons, who assist others that are sick, or injured. But when the mentally ill or homeless are allowed to sit with the congregation in a sanctuary or chapel to worship God, this plays a powerful role in healing. Sure, their appearance may not be upper-middle-class, but in their hearts, they are royalty, so to speak. One homeless man, the poorest man in the church, is extremely grateful for this opportunity to sit with Christ's royalty, the whole Christian congregation.

Marcia writes about faith in God as though her very life depends on it. And she believes that this is also the case for all of the other mentally ill. In Western culture, the medicalization of psychiatric illness did much to combat stigma; however, a religious view of what humans are made up of needs also to be addressed. Marcia has been working to present this perspective over the years. Spirituality is central to her writing, the human being composed of body, mind, and *spirit*. The secular world has dominated psychiatry for several hundred years, so progress depends on people of influence to stand up for the truth. Yes, medication is important, but at a minimal level. The biological is only one aspect of the puzzle. The mind, the nonmaterial aspect is dominant and the spirit of humans defines mental health. Without God, we'd all be dead. God gives us the air we breathe. God makes our heart beat. To acknowledge this, and to thank and love God is the first step in mental health. Marcia's early psychiatrist believed in this completely, and when Marcia wrote about it he supported her work. A strong theme throughout the literature is restoration of not only physical aspects as in repairing homelessness, but the emotional well-being of people who are mentally ill. Forgiveness is important. We need to ask forgiveness from God for all the wrongs we've done, and ask forgiveness from the individuals we've hurt. Without these steps, a person remains burdened, as though carrying a very heavy load.

This is the message we have heard from him and proclaim to you, that God is light and in him is no darkness at all. If we say we have fellowship with him while we walk in darkness, we lie and do not live according to the truth; but if we walk in the light, as he is in the light, we have fellowship with one another, and the blood of Jesus his Son cleanses us from all sin. If we say we have no sin, we deceive ourselves, and the truth is not in us. *If we confess our sins, he is faithful and just, and will forgive our sins and cleanse us from all unrighteousness.* If we say we have not sinned, we make him a liar, and his word is not in us. (1John 1: 5–10 RSV author's emphasis)

Worship services are valuable in their time of Confession of Sins section of the liturgy. The absolvent words: *You are forgiven,* are so important, I cannot stress it enough. Being made right with God, reconnected with God will bring much needed calm, peace, and healing. Sure, some physical handicap could remain with use of a wheelchair or crutches, but, mentally, forgiveness is necessary for good mental health. MHI stresses the need for restoration on a social level. Friendships are important. The literature has stories of exclusion and how hurtful this is for the mentally ill. As a person who has experienced this exclusion first hand, Marcia describes the challenges in keeping her faith amongst judgmental people. Thankfully, there are church members who are examples of Christ's love and compassion and who've provided friendship and also assistance on practical levels.

Marcia has written about trauma, and other personal experiences. Her psychiatrist wanted her to do this, saying it would bring healing, as well as provide insight for others who've never had the experience. Marcia's memoir is the story of her experience with mental illness through which she finds spiritual meaning and, ultimately, God. As a person who has experienced severe psychiatric illness and landed on her feet, she believes that she offers a unique first-person perspective. She tells what such illness is like, its symptoms, stigmatization, hospitalizations, and daily life. She takes you into her world where she found insights into the spiritual meaning of her illness. Her story may give desperately needed hope to others who are ill, their families, psychiatric professionals, as well as to those who know someone who is ill.

Another concept by Marcia that describes her view on mental illness is the following:

Generally speaking, many attribute mental health and illness solely to a physical material substance (the brain) without the spiritual attributes of the mind; they neglect the essence of being mentally healthy which is derived from the soul. They make false claims such as there being no progress in psychiatry for the past seven decades (not true); and casting aside any humility, want to remake something on a grand scale that comes from a limited, outside perspective (the objective observance of a professional), and, furthermore, from which they are drawing inaccurate conclusions.

It is common knowledge that in any field, the ambitious often try to make a name for themselves and with this ambition, will go to extremes. Most books on mental illness lack anything that Christians hold in the highest regard: the life of the spirit, the soul, the spiritual world (beings), human's utter dependence on God's sovereignty, and grace and protection, including Christ's role as healer by his witness through spoken testimony and acts recorded in the Holy Bible.

Marcia develops an understanding of mental illness using a biblical foundation as background, along with the lessons learned from the wisdom (and failures) of not only Western psychiatry, both currently and things gleaned over the past 300 years, but with the added depth of insights from the field of psychology and the vital contributions of religion. This will provide a holistic frame of reference and support a broader healing paradigm than one solely focused on a simple neurology of the physical brain. In addition, social milieus regarding familial and civic environments influence the myriad of mental troubles and Marica's writing addresses the micro aspect of one-on-one human interactions as well as macro connections within large communities. When trying to decipher causes of mental breakdown and what promotes healing, Marcia acknowledges the importance of good nutrition for the human body and brain, and hopeful thinking, but takes the reader further, through the complex picture of what moral, ethical, and value-based character looks like when speaking about a stable mental integrity. Mental integrity, a healthy mind, is what she is concerned about, and this can only be formed by adopting the God-given resources undergirding the Christian faith built upon biblical truths. A prudent psychiatry will recognize this and partner with those who are seeking to help patients develop a healthy character in tandem with logical and rational abilities. Right thinking, cognitive health, can dispel recurrent anxieties and other emotional problems because right thinking can promote a healthy lifestyle. Habits, patterns of healthy thinking, based on good values, will create a healthy life trajectory, leaving an unhealthy one behind;

and it all starts with acknowledging God as the redeemer, protector, and sustainer of a healthy life.

So, it is all material brain? Wrong diagnosis, wrong cure. Neurologists in isolation and taking human beings out of context, will not end mental illness because mental health and illness encompasses so much more than the mere neurological processes of the brain. We need God.

In Marcia's writing she often addresses the scientific community. She encourages mental health professionals to go beyond the biomedical model of brain dysfunction to consider the devastating impact of psychosis. She describes the psychotic symptoms she experienced as a young adult, problems she's had over the years, and factors that led to improvement in her condition. Marcia presents a thematic analysis of the meaning of psychosis. This is based on interviews she conducted with individuals who were taking part in a rehabilitation program. She asks the psychiatric community to consider these persons' interpretations of psychotic phenomena, and urges counselors, therapists, and doctors to recognize how spiritual attitudes and lifestyles give direction and meaning to the lives of those with psychiatric disabilities.

Marcia, team leader of MHI, is a Christian who has lived the life of a mental patient in the United States in the period between the closures of the big institutions in the 1950s and the advent of community care-based treatments. She provides an inside view of things as from someone who has much to say about the vital role of the church and society in counteracting the deplorable conditions faced by people who experience mental illness.

Marcia shares the story of how she became ill and what it was like to have a psychosis, post-traumatic stress disorder, and clinical depression. It is the story of how she found spiritual meaning—and ultimately, God—through her experience with mental illness.

Intrinsic to survival for the mentally ill is the question of meaning: meaning found in suffering and how it relates to religious faith. It's about how, without God, the Marcia feels she's be dead. Throughout much of her writing she describes how the church, though imperfect, has opened its doors to her, sharing the love of Christ in a myriad of ways, supporting her in her struggle to survive. Marcia's writing describes how difficult things are for individuals with mental illness. It is written for congregations, educators, health care professionals, civic leaders, government officials, and the general public. Not only can individuals become more sensitive to the needs of the mentally ill; but, consequently, this would systemically influence and improve society as a whole. Marcia's writing is some of the first to address the living conditions of the mentally ill from the standpoint of social justice. It is the first for religion to partner with the psychiatric field from a spiritual vantage point to improve the lives of those afflicted with medical, social, and spiritual maladies. It is written by someone who has lived with the challenges of a marginalized human being, someone who has insights that no one in the mainstream has experienced. Professionals often write from the viewpoint of someone observing their patients from the outside. Instead, Marcia tells what it feels like from the inside, to be afflicted with emotional, physical, and social challenges that hinder development and success. Marcia's writing offers solutions on many levels, unique by virtue of who and what she is as author: someone that has been in the darkest depths of severe distress and who found that Christ is the only hope for the mentally afflicted; and the church as Christ's body, though imperfect, has a vital role in healing and restoration.

Marcia describes the pain caused by stigmatization of the mentally ill. She shares her own experience of stigma as well as the experiences of those at the rehabilitation center where she conducted more interviews. She gives examples of discrimination and prejudice. She tells of how she found hope in the face of rejection, and how she believes mental health professionals and organizations can restore dignity to the lives of those with psychiatric illness. Finally, brethren, whatever is true, whatever is honorable, whatever is just, whatever is pure, whatever is lovely, whatever is gracious, if there is any excellence, if there is anything worthy of praise, think about these things. What you have learned and received and heard and seen in me, do; and the God of peace will be with you. (Phil 4: 7–9

RSV) And the peace of God, which passes all understanding, will keep your hearts and your minds in Christ Jesus.

Much of what Marcia has written is with the intention of promoting spirituality in medicine. Using a combination of personal account and theory, Marcia describes the transformative impact of psychosis. Standing alone, she feels the biomedical model of psychiatric illness is reductionistic. Instead, she believes a holistic view of mental illness is needed that merges secular psychiatry and religion. This validates the interconnectedness of body, mind, and spirit. She describes how adopting this perspective brought healing to her life. Marcia wrote about what any psychiatrist will tell you, that schizophrenia does not involve split or multiple personalities. This misconception has been fueled by the media and Hollywood. She explains that schizophrenia is a term that covers many kinds of symptoms such as, thought disorder, hallucinations (auditory or visual), delusions, apathy, and withdrawal. A person can have some or all of these and individual cases vary enormously. Marcia provides examples of activities that she undertook in the church which led to fellowship and a sense of well being. By involving herself in the religious community, she found that the love of Christ, through the Christian people, counteracts stigmatization that often breaks the heart and crushes the spirit of those with psychiatric disabilities.

With her writing, Marcia hopes to encourage rational thought and discussion about controversial topics with the hope that such reasoning and communications will result in greater understanding. She hopes to clarify various theological and philosophical positions that divide religious communities. Opposing camps often sit side by side on church pews. When we say we worship God what exactly is the focus of our worship? Can it matter to God as to who or what we think He/She is? Should it matter to us? What is the church? Who are God's people? Marcia's writing contains her reflections upon the apathetic condition of many who profess Christ. What does the Bible show God to be in regard to the afflicted, poor and oppressed? And, is the Christian community reflecting this God of the Bible and the example of Jesus Christ? Marcia also wrote something at the request of a person putting on a graduate school symposium on the topic of suicide. She wrote a letter to show the depth of problems that may compel a person toward suicidal thoughts and actions. These thoughts were her own, taken from her own experience. The answer from the therapist is authentic—her own therapist responded. Marcia touches upon other topics as well: Who can decide who is worthy of life or death? How do we judge a human being's worth? How do we treat those that society sees as weak and dependent? What is the Christian response? What is yours?

Here are some of Marcia's thoughts: Life is full of suffering. That is a truth no one can deny, whatever one's background. As a Christian I've learned that I can find meaning in suffering and in carrying my cross. But sometimes the sadness in my heart is so overpowering that my faith is challenged. I may question whether God really does love me. I may feel abandoned by family, friends, neighbors, and coworkers—utterly alone in the world. People with good intentions will recite verses to me about being still and knowing that God is there. Yet, they are often the ones with people around them, with spouses and children and grandchildren who comfort them. Most likely they, too, have experienced isolation during some point of their lives.

During the times I have felt lonely I have turned to history; to those who've gone before. I am led by an inner voice or compass that directs and guides me. These historical people are my friends and as I study their lives, mentors appear in my mind, touching my heart: feed the poor; liberate the oppressed; stand up for justice. I find this comforting God through books, films, photos, and I follow where God is leading me. My life unfolds by the inner workings of the Holy Spirit motivating and inspiring me to go forward—building on the foundations of those brave souls of the past who often spoke of a deep loneliness, but still doing what they could to further God's Kingdom.

Someone said that people with a mental illness are the lepers of modern day society. If this is true one may have felt rejected by those who appear socially successful. They have all the right college degrees, beautiful houses, fashionable clothes, and say all the right things. On the surface it looks like God has blessed them exclusively with abundance, wealth, health, and an easy life. But looking below the surface we may see signs of a deceptive self-sufficiency, self-perceived independence, and over-confidence—things that stand in the way of acknowledging God as their maker and sustainer, the one whom they need to depend on. To suffer from mental illness in all of its emotional trauma and very real challenges of not only physical deprivations, but also, social exclusion, can often bring one to one's knees. It is there that we find that Jesus Christ is all we have. It is our God who provides us with all that we need to live. It is God that sustains us. By joining with a religious community we can find acceptance in a concrete visible form of brothers and sisters in Christ who offer a helping hand. And like the leper that Christ reached out to and touched with compassion, we will be healed, finding a new life full of meaning and purpose. Under God's wings we will find shelter.

I don't know about you, but over the years I've had trouble with anger—and what to do with it. People have treated me badly, some because they don't like those with a mental illness. They may think we are all dumb, uneducated, lazy good for nothings. Our medications may cause weight gain so people think we overeat and lack self-discipline. When I've been abused I've asked God: "Why this curse?! Why do you hate me?! Did you give me my mental illness?! What have I done to deserve this punishment?! Answer me!!" Then I remember the story of the blind man in the Bible, who was born blind and Jesus said: "It is not because he sinned or his parents sinned that he was born blind. But he is blind so that the work of God might be displayed in his life." These words can soothe my soul and I can understand that all things work together for good if we love God. God can take the most painful, awful things and turn them into a positive force for the good. In the end, justice will prevail because God loves us.

I've heard that giving new life by physically giving birth to a child is no picnic. A parent working most days, all day long, to put food on the table for the family requires great emotional and physical sacrifice. When we look at our Lord God we see someone who cares for the poor, the outcasts, lame, and handicapped—those who our society deems unworthy of respect. We see around us the love of doctors caring for their patients; pastors watching over their flocks and teachers guiding their students. Though friends may desert us, there is someone who sticks closer than a brother. He died on a cross, suffering the humiliation of nakedness, with nails through his hands and feet. He experienced death so you and I would not have to. He took on God's wrath for the sinfulness of all humanity, suffering separation from God the Father so you and I could be united with God both here on earth and in Heaven through all eternity. Now, that's real love. No doubt about it.

The alternative of living for God is focusing on ourselves. If we love ourselves more than anything else, there is no room left to love others. People live in relation to others while on earth. It is impossible to avoid people. How we choose to live determines the quality of our spiritual life. To ignore the spiritual side is to live in a materialistic mindset. Then we seek fulfillment in fancy cars, but they do not satisfy; in sexual promiscuity, but find it destructive; in food and drink, but we never are satiated; in entertainment and self-gratification, but we end up feeling empty. If we as Christians believe that God is our sustainer and provider, then only through our connection to Him will we find all that we need: then relationships fall into place; our work is fulfilling; we find meaning in suffering and strength to endure. Without God, we sink into the depths of despair andfind no way out. But with the light of Christ, we find the path of peace, comfort and hope for the future.

We love God when we obey God. Emotions come and go. They are fleeting. How we conduct our lives says more. God gives His commands in the Bible, His word. In Exodus 20:1–17 we find the Ten Commandments. The New Testament lessons teach us how to obey. Through the parables and words of Christ and His followers, clear directions are given. They center around loving God and our neighbor. Who is our neighbor? All the people around us; no more, no less. We live by what our values dictate. Our values are displayed to the world by what we do. We choose our values by what we love. How we spend our time says what we love and therefore, value. We also become what we value because we worship what we value and become what we worship. We were created to worship God, the Holy Trinity: God the Father, Son, and Holy Spirit. We can learn what God is like and who He is by reading the Bible and seeing who Jesus Christ was in the New Testament. Asking God in prayer, "Who are you?" and "How can I know and understand my relationship with you?" is the beginning to knowing God and becoming like Him. We live by what is in our heads or, you could say—our minds. If we fill our minds with junk: violence, profanity, judgments, hatred, jealousy, greed, immorality, deceit, then these things are creating our personalities to reflect what the world will see in us. However, if we fill our minds with loving, healthy and pure thoughts like peace, loyalty, compassion, generosity, kindness, altruism, virtue, honesty, then this will become our personalities—what the world sees when it looks at us. The more we fill our minds with God's holy Word, the more we will be transformed to reflect God's nature.

GOD'S KINDNESS

I would like to tell of God's kindness which is what led me to found the Mental Health Initiatives ministry. It all started when I was an embryo inside my mother's womb. She didn't want me and tried to get support to get rid of me, but failed. So she carried me to term, gave birth, and I came into the world. I was unhappy as a child. My three siblings didn't want me either and tormented me with emotional abuse. But I found love in elementary school where teachers were kind to me. I would have been lost without the teachers. As I grew up I thought that if I looked attractive people would love me. But, instead, the opposite happened. I know now that people are repelled by the person who vainly focuses on outward beauty. Real beauty comes from within. Even though I attended a Lutheran church as a child and teenager with my family, I still got caught up later in an evil religious cult that worshiped a false god. While involved then in the cult, I became psychotic because I would pray to the cult's leader and this was worshipping an idol.

As I was becoming destroyed by the hallucinations which were frightening voices of demons, God reached out to me, to save me. In the middle of a rainstorm, the torrent of rain became a voice which said: "Believe in Jesus Christ and you'll be saved."

I tried to pray and eventually, I got help to leave the cult. As I arrived back home arrangements were made for me to be admitted into a psychiatric hospital as an inpatients. This was God's love and kindness. Since I was incapacitated by the psychosis and hallucinations, I needed help from healthcare providers. They gave me an antipsychotic, not too much and not too little, just the right amount. As I rested in that hospital, they gave me nourishing food because I was suffering from malnutrition. This was God's love and care. I was able to rest and sleep to try to regain some strength.

God was kind in also discharging me to a women's psychiatric halfway house. There were about six other women there all at various stages of recovery from mental illness. Here God provided rest and more nourishing food. I was able to socialize with the other tenants. My isolation was less but when I walked down the block to a church, I did worship there, but could not connect with the other people there. God led me to a Bible study group that was near the halfway house. I must have looked unusual because, again, probably from lack of social skills, I could not make any friends. But God, in his mercy, still guided me. I'd like to say that I had a big break but I didn't. For many years I struggled with difficult relationships and my biological family causes a lot of emotional turmoil. I struggled with employments. I struggled in poverty. God blessed me with a series of apartments. They were mostly substandard, but I coped. At the peak of (or rather, at the bottom of) despair, I nearly succeeded in ending my own life. By a miracle, I made it to the ER in time and then was hospitalized for a couple of weeks, partly in the ICU. I left the hospital AMA (going against doctor's advice). Again, God took care of me, he was kind. I remembered the voice in the rain and went to a church three walking blocks away. I put all my faith in that voice I felt in my heart was God's voice. This began a journey through the

Presbyterian Church (USA). God gave me a chance again, which was God's kindness.

I was not immediately accepted by this congregation. In order to be socially engaged and in order to learn God's word, I joined a Bible study. Soon after, I started doing volunteer work by collating the church newsletter, helping to get it ready for a mailing. People were kind. In the Bible study the women were cautious and didn't really want to be friends with me. But I kept going to the study once a week for approximately twelve years. I did learn a lot about the Bible during these twelve years and I did set-up of the coffee and chairs. I felt God's love and kindness as I tried to be a part of this group. It soon became apparent that I needed more structure and a different kind of volunteer work, so I went elsewhere, to a medical facility. And I started writing. God eventually, in his kindness helped me to get a used computer, and a college instructor offered to set up a website for me to display my work. I went online and my whole life changed. I could now explore the internet and converse with hundreds of people through email. My isolation was less. This was God's kindness. But unfortunately, my body had a lot of health issues and my physical pain was extreme. It was difficult to walk. I was bleeding. But I kept writing as much as I could anyway, and things started to get published. My contacts grew to even talking with professors online. This was God's kindness. My food scarcity still kept me malnourished, however, and I struggled to make ends meet. I remember being hungry a lot. My biological family didn't help, but, instead, tormented me. My psychiatrist advised me to stay away from them, so I did as much as possible.

My psychiatrist, Dr. Russell Noyes, Jr, was kind. This was God's kindness to me, having someone there in my life who provided stability and support. Give justice to the weak and the fatherless; maintain the right of the afflicted and the destitute. Rescue the weak and the needy; deliver them from the hand of the wicked." (Psalm 82:3–4 RSV)

I increased my writing projects and wrote more articles and books. I gave presentations. My social contacts grew in number. I still had some psychotic symptoms, however, and a sleep disorder.

My female friends were few in number and the male boyfriend mistreated me. My housing situation became unbearable, then God, in his mercy, gave me a new home in a nice apartment building, and I was able to get more food, also. My work in MHI started when I was writing the articles about the topic of faith being important in recovery from mental illness and I started bring new, clean bath towels to the old homeless shelter in town on the north side. I worked as a volunteer at the city's Free Lunch serving meals to the homeless, mentally ill, and other poor.

God, in his kindness, gave me people along the way who advised me and encouraged me to write more and to work as an advocate for those with mental illness. I've accompanied one homeless man to the court house when he was erroneously summoned for jury duty. I explained to the clerk of court, that this was a mistake because my friend was mentally and physically disabled and homeless, and it was impossible for him to serve on jury duty. They quickly corrected it. If I had not helped him by going with him to the court house and explained things to the clerk, he would have eventually been arrested and put in jail because of being unable to comply. You may wonder how he received mail if he is homeless. There is a system set up in the city to help with this.

God's kindness is evident by the loving people that came into my life. As a person with mental illness, I've had a lot of needs. God brought a friend to me who saw I needed food, and brought me groceries. And when I injured my shoulder, another friend brought food. I was unable to purchase a vacuum cleaner because of the expense, but a person from church did it for me with hers on numerous occasions. If the church really wants to assist the mentally ill, they could ask them what kind of help they need most. Sometimes, it is coffee times with conversation. Sometimes, it is lunch out. Often, a text or email is a great help. MHI has team members who do this type of thing for others. God's kindness is expressed when Christian people greet others out in public, even just a "hello, how are you doing?" This can mean a great deal for a person with mental illness. Psychiatrists who speak in a kind tone of voice, nonjudgmentally, are a big help. When the doctor is harsh and the voice reflects this, a patient with mental illness will lose hope. Psychiatrists need to instill hope. Kindness goes a long way. I cannot stress this enough.

God's love came to me in the form of a good friend. Just because a person with mental illness may have some emotional or psychological problems occasionally, doesn't mean they aren't loving, caring persons. This person who is a good friend has been diagnosed with schizophrenia and he is also physically disabled. However, he does anything he can to protect me, to keep me safe from harm, and to help me get everything I need for daily life. He loves God, he says. "Where is God?" I ask him. "God is invisible," he says, "God is with us here, and is always with us."

ADVOCATES IN HEALTHCARE

You would think that people who go into the medical field would be compassionate human beings because they want to help suffering people, right? That's not always the case. Many people with a psychiatric diagnosis are systematically mistreated and discriminated against on a regular basis. Once your medical chart lists *schizophrenia or bipolar*, you are someone doomed for life. Marcia accompanied a gentleman who has schizophrenia to his psychiatric appointment one day. After checking in, we sat in the waiting room for the doctor. The med tech did his vitals quickly down the hall, so that went okay. But the wait for the psychiatrist went on and on, for an inordinate amount of time. It was so long, I approached the receptionist to ask if the doctor was even aware of my friend's presence. She assured me he was aware. So, finally, after a very long time, the doctor called my friend without giving an apology, and down the hall they went to the office. But that's not all. My friend, after the appointment ended, chose to share with me what went on. After the psychiatrist in the office asked my friend two or three brief questions, the doctor turned his back on his patient and resumed working on his computer, typing away, scrolling, until thirty minutes were up and back out the door they went and down the hall. Clearly, this was subpar treatment. First, my friend, a child-like innocent human being had placed full confidence in this doctor only to be treated disrespectfully. Making the patient wait for copious amounts of time in the waiting room is not considerate, to say the least. It's giving the message: *You are not important or worthy of my time.* And when the doctor only spoke briefly in the office and turned his back and worked on his computer, it goes without saying, how rude, and hurtful this would be for a patient. Again, it gives the message: *You are not important or worthy of my time.* And on it goes. There are complaints of physicians being impatient with a person with a mental illness diagnosis, being short-tempered, angry at them. Not giving the patient choices in their own care. Not being given explanations about diagnosis or options for treatments. All around bad care. Sometimes, you will hear the providers laughing about patients and mocking them. The MHI advocate will stand with their friends who suffer such abuse.

DISTRIBUTION OF MATERIALS

Who reads the MHI literature that Marcia writes, besides some of the membership in churches? MHI has a website, www.hopeforrecovery.com, which is international, and also MHI team members mail out flyers and provides free copies of the books to the local libraries, Christian Counseling Centers, and Christian University Libraries on the local, state, and national levels. To mail out these things, it takes time. First, MHI creates labels of the addresses of each facility or organization. Internet searches provide the names, addresses, and general accessibility. The labels are printed out and cut to size, then taped onto envelopes or packages. MHI team members work together on these projects. This is a fun activity and provides structure to the day, and purposeful joy. When the people on the receiving end respond in gratitude the MHI work is validated. There are people with mental illness who will send emails; therapists from counseling centers, and even professors who give positive feedback. Christian pastors have phoned to ask for advice regarding parishioners who attend their church who struggle with mental illness. Sometimes difficult behaviors are addressed or issues regarding social inclusion and integration. Many people express gratitude for receiving flyer notices of the MHI books or hard copies because this kind of writing is so new for a secular world, and even in the church. Religious bodies are strengthened knowing that the spiritual perspective of mental illness, being ignored for so long, is now coming to the fore. Instinctively, people know God is to be at the center of our lives, or even more importantly, the mental life. And when they find literature that validates this, a flyer in the mail, or book, steps are taken to increase the mental health of the whole church community or congregation, as well as, the surrounding, broader civic community. The ideas and concepts of the written literature increased hope exponentially, outward and inward.

PSYCHIATRIC PATIENTS' APPAREL PROGRAM

Book sale proceeds go to supply clothing, shoes, and other needed items for homeless, and low-or-no-income psychiatric patients in a hospital setting. MHI set up a fund entirely for this purpose (2019); its called the Psych Patients' Apparel Program. For several years, since 2009, Marcia had been spearheading clothing drives to collect sweat pants for psychiatric in-patients at the University of Iowa Hospitals & Clinics [UIHC]. The nursing staff had identified this need for suitable, comfortable clothing as sometimes the medications can cause weight gain and better physical comfort allows patients to focus on improving their mental health. Many patients are homeless, low-income, come from out of state and/or lack family support. This caring program had been well-received, but the need outweighed the supply and practical considerations of storage, moving clothing, and matching sizes complicated the process. In an effort to more efficiently reach a greater number of patients, Marcia worked with the UI Center for Advancement to set up a fund within the UI Psychiatry Department to allow for the purchase of apparel items, mainly sweatpants, tops, and shoes (and seasonal outerwear–coats), for inpatients whom the nurses identify as needing this service.

MHI was grateful to the church congregation for its past support with physical items and moved on to monetary donations. Most people know of someone who suffers from a mental illness and how it causes disruptions to all segments of society which are costly, not only monetarily, but emotionally and socially. Helping the psychiatric patients gain a stronger foothold once again in a hospital setting can often be life-saving because many patients are suicidal. Marcia knows this because she was there, in a psych ward, and penniless. She owned only the shirt on her back. Marcia's biological family was not helpful. She depended on strangers. Marcia was diagnosed with schizophrenia, she heard voices, demonic and one, appearing to be divine. The psych ward, (or psych unit) protected her for the time being after escaping a bad cult that had her selling flowers, candy, and candles for the leader's financial gain. She was driven out in the bitter cold, and the heat of summer for this fundraising so the leaders of the cult could become very wealthy. She had sleepless nights trying to rest on wooden floors, traveling in the cult vans cross-country in groups of seven or eight. Malnourished, the psych unit was now a place that provided food to help her rebuild her strength. They gave her antipsychotic medication. It seemed to help. She tried to rest. Being all alone in the world, her reflections on her past life made little sense. The staff came across as kind and compassionate except for one nurse who didn't believe Marcia when she told her that she was hearing voices. Marcia was terrified because the voices were horrific and loud and belligerent. It took several months as an in-patients there before Marcia could be released to a psychiatric half-way house for females. And she was given out-patient care by the psychiatrist who would eventually encourage her writing. Marcia tried to work at employment several times, but each time, her emotional problems, and desperate housing situation, and food scarcity made it impossible to sustain work. She also did volunteer work. Marcia had MHI set up this Psych Patient Apparel Fund because she knows, first hand, what it is like to struggle with a severe mental illness, to be without family support, and be too sick to hold down employment, thus being unable to take care of basic needs. She's lived with cockroaches, mice, spiders, leaking pipes, broken heating and A/C systems, predatory and bullying neighbors, people banging on the walls, threats, gunshots outside bedroom windows in the middle of the night, and much, much more. She's known physical and emotional assaults and abuse, lack of safety in general, and the sleepless nights that go with it. So, yes, she empathizes with the psych patients who have nothing, and not even clothes to wear. Who are at the bottom and need a helping hand. Where would Marcia be without the health professionals who gave her a helping hand when she needed it? She'd be dead, most likely. Where would Marcia have been without the hospitals? Out on the streets, homeless, and hungry.

Marcia, through MHI, set up this Psych Patients' Apparel Fund; and, hopefully, others will see the need to assist those down on their luck and provide financial support. We're all in this together. The so-called, *healthy and successful* are only a traffic accident away from disaster or losing a home, a relative, or one's own health. As a friend of mine once said who runs a medical clinic: *There is no cure for death.* And I might add, or disaster. Tornados, floods, fire, cancer, job loss, blindness, you name it, no cures for most of those. Marcia recovered sufficiently to the point where she could take steps to aid others who need assistance, so this clothing fund/program, an outgrowth of MHI will assist people in getting back on their feet. And as they say, it's a ripple effect, a growth going outward and beyond the self.

Marcia writes small grant applications for funding. Marcia learned how to apply for funding through a volunteer job. In this job, she wrote small applications or requests for items to assist people who had mental illness. They were all approved. She also increased her computer skills at this job that eventually improved her writing abilities technically. The other volunteers when engaging in conversation where helping Marcia, though unknowingly, to increase Marcia's social skills. She was a late bloomer, learning what most people learn in high school or junior high. Also, in addition, what increased Marcia's verbal skills, a doctor invited Marcia to give presentations for nursing staff and medical students beginning in 2006. This speaking went on for twelve years. She eventually gave PowerPoint talks with colorful slides. MHI claims these years of speaking as productive knowledge-and experience-sharing years. It was not easy because Marcia was not a very verbal person previously. The talks gave her a measure of confidence when talking with others. MHI was spreading information in healthcare setting to future or current care providers with the hope of increasing compassion for the mentally ill and those who struggle in other ways related to mental illness. Later, Marcia did applications at various places for funding to support the Apparel Fund. The financial support came from individual church members and at the Presbytery level, as well as religious communities within the local area.

ENRICHING ONE-ON-ONE CONVERSATIONAL DIALOGUES AND LISTENING OPPORTUNITIES

Much can be said regarding the value of humans conversing with one another, especially if it is done in a respectful manner. But far too often we find hurtful gossip and negative comments behind other's backs. MHI takes a different view, that of building each other up. MHI members seek out those who may be lonely or isolated and engages the person in conversation. This can be done in person or on the phone, or through emails and greeting cards. Marcia phones a woman who is near seventy years old every day, sometimes twice a day. This person is a near shut in, going out only for groceries. This person confided in Marcia that she was diagnosed with schizophrenia aa a young adult. Now she mainly sits in her house and watches TV and reads her Bible. I asked her why she doesn't call any of her church friends. She attends a church on Sunday. She said, "If someone wants to talk to me, they will call me." So, she is isolated. She will tell me that she did her laundry on Monday and cleaned the church on Thursday. Other than that, along with a church group meeting on Wednesday, she sits alone in her house. My presence for her over the phone is a way to support her. I try to engage her in conversation but usually, she just responds with a "yes, or "no." I suggest for her to take a walk, especially on bright, sunny days. I ask her how she's doing and is there anything on her mind or anything she wants to talk about? She also has a physical disability that hampers her mobility so she uses a cane. Rarely, will she use city mass transit. Her acquaintances from church know that she is isolated, and a few respond by taking her out to lunch, but this is not enough. She sits alone in her house every day. When I call her she is very cordial and kind. I can sense her gratitude for the contact I've made. But it isn't all one sided. She also supports me with her own presence. I'm grateful to hear her voice and feel useful by supporting her. MHI has value in the act of supporting the outcast, those rejected by the world. People with mental illness can see the rejection in other people's faces, their judgmental eyes. People with mental illness may be kicked out of coffee shops or stores, or hounded and badgered by store security staff. They may be accused of illegal activities such as shop lifting when all they want to do is look around the store. People who have mental illness may be more likely to be arrested than others because of an unkempt appearance. So when MHI members visit them or call them on the phone, this encourages them. Can you imagine being alone for twenty-four hours or longer? It's like solitary confinement. This damages the brain. It can cause forms of dementia. Cognitive abilities are harmed by isolation and some people never recover.

Another person Marcia supports in the MHI way is a man I'll call Jon. He sits downtown on a bench most days except in the dead of winter. He is homeless and his few belongings are stacked up beside him. For many years Marcia has stopped by to ask, "How's it going?" He responds, "Oh, it's going!" Marcia has shared with him where a free church meal is available. She has asked him about going to the Iowa City Free Lunch on the bus. She found out that for a short time period someone let him sleep in the person's van at night. But that arrangement didn't last more than a few months. During frigid weather, Marcia noticed he was outside. Approaching him, she asked if he was doing okay. He said he wanted to try to get back into the shelter system, he had previously been evicted.

I said that I would talk to them. Marcia spoke with a shelter staff and arranged for a shelter outreach person to go downtown to talk to Jon to encourage him to go to the winter shelter where he would be allowed in. He was always welcome there.

MHI supports people who need emotional bonding. Some have rejected psychiatric assistance and are going it alone, without medication, or therapy. Their symptoms make it very difficult to converse with others or act normally. Often they might scurry away in fear. Some people are very meek and feel nobody would want to get to know them. So they sort of hide. When MHI sees a person who is isolated in a group setting, this is something we like to attend to. Marcia hopes by her talking to them that they can feel welcome, especially, at church events.

MHI team members get together, mostly one-on-one meetings. We talk about justice issues and things pertaining to mental health and the homeless. Recently, the state legislature wanted to make things too difficult for the homeless shelters to remain open with a proposed bill. MHI members care about this. Marcia and a team member got together and prayed for God to protect the shelters. This team member is important for the conversations of what MHI can do in the future with the literature, or holding events. She had the skills and was essential for coordinating a Zoom event with a professor who discussed the problem of bullying in the schools. Other team members are also essential to the MHI organization. Touching base on Sundays at church gives us support and strength. We discuss the Initiatives and plans for our work. Some of us pray for our work to succeed. Email conversations are important also. And Texting. The MHI team values one another and we respect our differences, feeling we can all learn from our different perspectives.

YARN CRAFTS

One of the MHI activities is knitting, crocheting, or looming blankets or prayer socks. The blankets are donated to the homeless shelter where there are many individuals who suffer from mental afflictions and challenges. A shelter staff said they all have a mental illness. The shelter staff express enthusiastic gratefulness. We are welcomed when an MHI team member drops off the donations. These blankets are made with loving hands, and prayerful hearts. The homeless person is allowed to take their own blanket with them when they leave the shelter and move into their own home. MHI hopes the blankets will comfort them and support a hopeful outlook because the situation of being homeless is extremely traumatic and life altering. The act of creating the colorful blankets is also healthy for the MHI team member. Doing yarn craft projects is good for the brain, a good brain exercise. So, it's a win–win situation, good for us and also the person receiving our gift of love.

Prayer socks created by an MHI team member are often on display at church events. We ask for a donation in exchange for a pair of socks. These are lovingly done with the team member praying for the recipient. Prayer is very powerful so this is a worthwhile activity that supports the mentally ill. The proceeds go into the Psych Patients' Apparel Program (previously mentioned).

TECHNOLOGY AND VIDEOS

To edify and uplift the church body as well as market the MHI books, Marcia has been graciously supported by a church staff who knows the technology for creating videos and is a real expert. Over the years, they have worked together describing books, projects, and events. This staff person is an extremely talented individual who has generously spent many hours on and off the clock making sophisticated, complex, and appealing videos that, with Marcia, describe books she has written and events taken place. This kind of technological assistance is invaluable for any church mental health ministry. Sometimes, other MHI team members play a part in the production of the videos by providing their voice narration with the reading of a script written by Marcia. MHI has discussed the problem of bullying in a Zoom program that gathered numerous people online. Team members who had the tech skills ran this event and it was highly successful.

PRAYER

Psychiatric patients, themselves, will need to take responsibility for their road to healing. And prayer allows for such lasting healing to take place. Marcia, of MHI, offers up this prayer:

Heavenly Father, we pray for those who suffer from mental illness, addictions, homelessness, and starvation. May those who have much, help those who have little. We pray for generous hearts of compassion. We pray that families can love one another with little strife. We pray that mothers can love their children and fathers be good and kind. We pray that all children will feel welcomed into this world and be supported with loving kindness. We pray that children everywhere will be taught the golden rule, to treat others the same way we would like to be treated. We pray for an end to bullying whether in the home or school, or workplace, an end to gossip and hurtful words. And that the church can be made conscious of the power of words and use words wisely. We pray that all you children, Lord, can have what they need to survive, adequate food, clothing, and shelter throughout their entire lives. That they can know the love of Christ through the ministers of your word and sacrament. We pray that healers will reach out to the sick, those with mental afflictions, and guide with wisdom and patience. We pray for the healthcare providers to be kind toward all people, especially, the poor, homeless and disenfranchised. We pray that law makers will have compassion in their hearts and do nothing to harm the homeless mentally ill, but pass laws to build up instead. We pray for the church leaders to govern the religious communities with fairness and equity. We pray that the congregations will open their hearts and minds to greater understanding of the poor and those who've struggled with employment, to refrain from judgment. Righteous Father, by the gracious power of the Holy Spirit, enlighten those in the ancient darkness of additions and violence, in prison cells, and in jails. Give us new opportunities to reform and be transformed, made new. Help us, Lord, to all know the love of Christ, his helpful hand. Where there is anger, Lord, bring calm. Where there is hatred, help us to love one another. Where there is confusion, bring clarity. Where there is hopelessness, bring us the light of redemption. Lord, may all your people be protected from the power of the evil one. May those who don't know you, find the path of light. May those in bars and back alleys be set free from their harmful lifestyles. May people with sexual problems be set free from destructive ways of living. That the marriage bed be honored by all and that adultery be rejected in favor of honesty, loyalty, and true love. We pray that those who hear voices can find that the voice of the church beckons even louder where they can find safety, God's strong protection. May we all recognize our own weakness, moral, emotional, and physical, and humble ourselves to the point where we recognize that we need God and his mercy, we can't go it alone. May all people see that mental illness touches all our lives in some form, whether in our own anxieties and fears, or in an over-blown ego, arrogance, and pride. We know that the devil's sin was pride, and we all have a tendency to inflate our own importance. We repent for competing against one another whether academically, socially, financially, or physically. Give us humble hearts full of humility. Let us build each other up and give support to one another knowing that the greatest form of love is to speak the truth to one another. Forgive us, Lord, for our idols and help us turn away from them. Give us sound theology in our churches, the truth, not worship of the creature. Forgive us for putting your creatures before you, almighty God, because we are to love you, Lord, more than anyone or anything. And you give us the truth to guide us out of the darkness of sin and death. Help us to repent of our wicked ways, to ask for forgiveness and therefore, receive your mercy and a new start in life. We need new beginnings. Lord, so many times we have insulted you by our rebellion. Guide us to the way everlasting. Take away our adulterous hearts and give us faithfulness to your word and holy way of life. Deep in our hearts we know we can't live without you. If we stray, bring us back. If we fall, lift us back up. Nothing matters more except being in right relationship with you. Help us, Lord, to get our priorities straight, guide us. Give us wise leadership in the church, in the field of medicine, and in government. Help the landlords to have compassion for the poor, to decrease the cost of rent. Help those who struggle with bullying neighbors to find safety. In psychiatry, give the therapists wisdom to know how to help their patients, to be loving and kind always. If someone is suicidal, Lord, please give them hope of a better future. Help people know that things can and often do change for the better. With some effort, people can take steps to help themselves. Give us, Lord, right perspectives. And when we differ in opinions with our neighbors, give us patience to listen. Almighty Father, giver of life, lead us out of the ancient darkness. Help us to shun the illicit drugs and alcohol, to look for a better way to find happiness and enjoyment in life. If we idolize money, guide us to find ways to use it to help others. If we have plenty of food, give us hearts to share it with others. Lord, people with mental illness have been rejected by family, neighbors, religious communities, medical providers, and business leaders. Have mercy on our souls. Help us to find acceptance and social integration. Help the mentally ill to find the love of Christ. With Christ's love comes healing and restoration. Give Christians the wisdom to know how to help others find the truth, and the way. Help those who don't believe in God to have faith. And finally, give us the heart to never leave you, Lord, to never betray you, for with you is life everlasting and eternal. Amen.

Conclusion

THE MINISTRIES OF MINDS Matter and Mental Health Initiatives (MHI) add depth and scope to congregations, surrounding communities, and organizations that are made up of a mix of people with complex individual needs. These organizations promote greater understanding of mental illness and health and related issues like poverty, and stigma, and they increase social integration.

When much of the secular world rejects those who have a mental illness, where are they to turn? People who have a mental illness are often living in poverty because they are rejected by potential employers. Who wants to hire a schizophrenic? Or someone who's been incarcerated? Indeed, many of those with mental illness wind up in prisons or jails because of minor offenses like trespassing. The homeless have nowhere to go and end up arrested. Employers won't give them a chance to prove themselves. So without a job, it's difficult to purchase nice or appropriate clothing. When they are out in public, people shun them because of their shabby appearance. Where can they find a shower and get themselves cleaned up? How can the mentally ill get treatment when the only medication prescriber at a clinic, they are told, comes in once a month, and they don't know which day, or the time of day, or for how long, and the waiting list for treatment is mile long.

MHI promotes the healthy activity of work. Team members have projects that increase social interaction and cooperation. Some of the team have never experienced mental illness and there are some who have. Some are retired, senior persons. Others are younger. Being productive gives a person a sense of meaning and purpose if they feel the work is worthwhile. Advocating for others gives a person a sense of accomplishment. The MHI work has a far reaching affect. Marcia can see on her website stats page how people from all across the US and in Europe, Asia, and other parts of the world read her articles and books. The MHI work crosses boundaries of race, ethnicity, culture, and language.

BEING AN ADVOCATE: A WORD FROM THE AUTHOR

I know we need advocates for those who have a mental illness because I have experienced discrimination firsthand. Being a writer, I have done a lot of research for projects so have spent time in libraries. I won't name the institution, but one day I was hounded and followed around a library as I was searching for a book in the stacks. I didn't look like your typical teenage or young adult, upper middle-class college student. I was middle-age, used crutches, and was dressed modestly, more like lower class. It could also have been discrimination against the handicapped since I was mobility-impaired and needed to use crutches. When I saw this badgering going on as though I was about to be kicked out of the library for no reason, I decided to send a complaint to the library administration and did. A person there did a follow-up and said she would take some steps to remedy the situation with her over-zealous staff. Apparently, they have security people that go too far.

This kind of thing happens to any person of modest means who can't afford expensive clothing, purses, or bags. And this is more like to occur with people who have a psychiatric illness because many of us are poor people. This is one reason education is important and the MHI literature can make a difference. People who read the MHI publications may become more understanding, be more accepting, and welcoming. There will be less stigma.

> Give the king thy justice, O God,
> and thy righteousness to the royal son!
> May he judge thy people with righteousness,
> and thy poor with justice!

Let the mountains bear prosperity for the people,
  and the hills, in righteousness!
May he defend the cause of the poor of the people,
  give deliverance to the needy,
  and crush the oppressor!

May he live while the sun endures,
  and as long as the moon, throughout all generations!
May he be like rain that falls on the mown grass,
  like showers that water the earth!
In his days may righteousness flourish,
  and peace abound, till the moon be no more!

May all kings fall down before him,
  all nations serve him!

For he delivers the needy when he calls,
  the poor and him who has no helper.
He has pity on the weak and the needy,
  and saves the lives of the needy.
From oppression and violence he redeems their life;
  and precious is their blood in his sight.
(Psalm 72: 1–7, 11–14 RSV)

When the church recognizes the dilemma and hopeless situation that engulfs a mentally ill person's daily life, many step in to assist. There are food pantries, clothing drives, prayer groups, along with individualswho offer other forms of care, such as transportation assistance. The ministries supporting those afflicted with mental illness and their families are game changers. They are run by people who have their own unique gifts and talents essential for the task. Minds Matter ministry increases visibility and spreads awareness of organizations and other information vital for mental health recovery and which is also helpful for relatives and/or coworkers of those who suffer. The speakers they have provide important information not easily found elsewhere. Mental Health Initiatives (MHI) ministry was created by a person who is in recovery from severe mental illness. She can and does identify in this book things she knows are most helpful for the ill, those who've lost everything to psychiatric illness. These two ministries were possible because of a compassionate church made up of people who care about others, who decided to invest in events and projects geared to increase stability and health for those afflicted by mental illnesses. Maybe they know someone afflicted or maybe someone in their family is sick; either way, the ministries described in this book give hope to the hopeless within church building walls and beyond. St. Andrew Presbyterian Church of Iowa City, has Elders, Deacons, and Staff who want to support those with psychiatric illness, their families, and friends. Thank you. Generous funding is provided for the volunteer work to continue year after year. The MHI ministry has been sustained for many years, along with the newer Minds Matter ministry. Various pastors have read Marcia's manuscripts and provided endorsements. When the homeless need a warm jacket or sturdy shoes, pastors generously provide them through the Deacon's Fund which is made possible by individual members of the church. Thank you. When there have been controversial beliefs or conversations, it is worked out. Nobody likes conflict. People listen to one another to try to understand. Feedback is appreciated and corrections are made. If feelings get hurt, we apologize for wrong doing and continue forward. Worshipping God together at services is priority for what brings us together in unity. We love God and strive to love one another. We know this goes together. Thank you.

Glory to God!

> He who dwells in the shelter of the Most High,
> who abides in the shadow of the Almighty,
> will say to the Lord, "My refuge and my fortress;
>   my God, in whom I trust."
> For he will deliver you from the snare of the fowler
>   and from the deadly pestilence;
> he will cover you with his pinions,
>   and under his wings you will find refuge;
>   his faithfulness is a shield and buckler.
> You will not fear the terror of the night,
>   nor the arrow that flies by day,

nor the pestilence that stalks in darkness,
nor the destruction that wastes at noonday.

A thousand may fall at your side,
ten thousand at your right hand;
but it will not come near you.
You will only look with your eyes
and see the recompense of the wicked.

Because you have made the Lord your refuge,
the Most High your habitation,
no evil shall befall you,
no scourge come near your tent.

For he will give his angels charge of you
to guard you in all your ways.
On their hands they will bear you up,
lest you dash your foot against a stone.
You will tread on the lion and the adder,
the young lion and the serpent you will trample under foot.

Because he cleaves to me in love, I will deliver him;
I will protect him, because he knows my name.
When he calls to me, I will answer him;
I will be with him in trouble,
I will rescue him and honor him.
With long life I will satisfy him,
and show him my salvation.
Psalm 91:1–16 RSV

Appendix

Further Reading

Books by Marcia A. Murphy

Founder, Mental Health Initiatives
Group for the Advancement of Mental Health

Murphy, Marcia A. *Faith & Major Mental Illness: Stories, Meditations, and Essays.* Eugene: Resource Publications, an imprint of Wipf & Stock Publishers, 2025.

Author's book webpage: https://hopeforrecovery.com/faith-major-mental-illness-stories-meditations-and-essays-by-marcia-a-murphy/

Murphy, Marcia A. *Concerning the Importance of God for Mental Health: Religious Faith and Its Relationship to Long-Term Cognitive, Emotional, and Behavioral Outcomes.* Eugene: Resource Publications, an imprint of Wipf & Stock Publishers, 2025.

Author's book webpage: Concerning the Importance of God for Mental Health

Murphy, Marcia A. *Knitting with Barbed Wire: Understanding the Factor of Religion in Mental Illness & Health.* Eugene: Resource Publications, an imprint of Wipf & Stock Publishers, 2024.

Author's book webpage: Knitting with Barbed Wire: Understanding the Factor of Religion in Mental Illness & Health by Marcia A. Murphy

Murphy, Marcia A. *The Compassionate Psychiatrist: Redefining Mental Healthcare.* Eugene: Resource Publications, an imprint of Wipf & Stock Publishers, 2024.

Author's book webpage: The Compassionate Psychiatrist by Marcia A. Murphy

Murphy, Marcia A. *Homeless: The Unbefriended Poor.* Eugene: Resource Publications, an imprint of Wipf & Stock Publishers, 2023.

Author's book webpage: Homeless

Murphy, Marcia A. *Schizophrenia & Suicide: Finding Hope, Meaning, and Direction.* Eugene: Resource Publications, an imprint of Wipf & Stock Publishers, 2023.

Author's book webpage: Schizophrenia & Suicide: Finding Hope, Meaning, and Direction by Marcia A. Murphy

Murphy, Marcia A. *A Small Handbook of Mental Health: Portal to a New Life.* Eugene: Resource Publications, an imprint of Wipf & Stock Publishers, 2022.

Author's book webpage: Small Handbook of Mental Health

Murphy, Marcia A. *Reflections on the Meaning of Mental Integrity: Recovery from Serious Mental Illness.* Eugene: Resource Publications, an imprint of Wipf & Stock Publishers, 2021.

Author's book webpage: https://wipfandstock.com/9781666708899/reflections-on-the-meaning-of-mental-integrity/

Murphy, Marcia A. *The Collected Writings of Marcia A. Murphy: Christus Magnus Medicus Sanat (Christ, the Great Physician,*

Heals). Eugene: Resource Publications, an imprint of Wipf & Stock Publishers, 2020.

Author's book webpage: https://hopeforrecovery.com/collected-writings/

Murphy, Marcia A. *To Loose the Bonds of Injustice: The Plight of the Mentally Ill and What the Church Can Do.* Eugene: Resource Publications, an imprint of Wipf & Stock Publishers, 2018.

Author's book webpage: https://www.hopeforrecovery.com/to-loose-the-bonds-of-injustice/

ALLBOOKS REVIEW INTERNATIONAL EDITOR'S CHOICE AWARD FOR 2011 FINALIST

Murphy, Marcia A. *Voices in the Rain: Meaning in Psychosis.* Cedar Rapids, IA: Eagle Book Bindery, 2010. Eugene: Wipf & Stock Publishers, Reprint 2018.

Author's book webpage: https://www.hopeforrecovery.com/voices-rain-meaning-psychosis/

www.ingramcontent.com/pod-product-compliance
Lightning Source LLC
LaVergne TN
LVHW010545100826
845148LV00013B/2606

* 9 7 9 8 3 8 5 2 7 6 4 9 3 *